£3

C000261165

This collection is dedicated to
my mother Margaret
my brother Jordan
my wife Sara
and
is in memory of
my father Thomas

Contents

NEW POEMS

Introduction

I first heard Todd Swift read his poetry at the Bowery Poetry Club in New York City in October 2002, just after the publication of his second collection, *Café Alibi*. I purchased a copy of *Café Alibi* that evening and it is one of those rare poetry collections I find myself returning to again and again. What most impressed me at the time was the stylish way his poems have of saying quite disturbing things. In his relentless efforts to get at the truth, Swift always works with the scalpel, never the sledgehammer. In this sense, his is an excellent example for younger poets with lots to say, but still on the lookout for the exact words in the exact order.

Back in 2002, at thirty-five years of age, I wasn't exactly young, but I was very much a poet in search of the exact words in the exact order. Swift's example had a profound influence at what was a crucial time for me as an emerging poet. In many ways, without once trying to persuade me of anything, he fundamentally altered my view of what poetry could be.

The British critic, Al Alvarez, writing about his fourth collection, *Winter Tennis* (2007), claims that his "work is always blessedly, unashamedly elitist." Maybe. But Swift is the right kind of elitist, if indeed he is one. He is a connoisseur of the best in poetry internationally, and his own work reflects a longstanding engagement with excellence. In several of the poems in *Café Alibi,* such as "Sheer Speculation" and "The More Deserved", both

11

of which are included here, he nods in the direction of Larkin.

Swift writes about disappointment and alienation with such beautiful understatement. That said, he is certainly not of the "heaven knows I'm miserable now" school. A poet can't really know the darkness without also knowing the light. Forster once wrote that "beside the eternal Why? there is a Yes and a Yes and a Yes." "Water, Running", an exquisite poem about the poet's marriage, is an offering to precisely that eternal Yes.

Todd Swift is a skilled practitioner of the short accessible lyric, certainly. But he is more than that. One of the striking things about his work is the multiplicity of his influences (some of them quite post-modern—he also sometimes sounds like an updated Muldoon, or Bernstein). In his essay, "What I Do Best, What I Do Now", which appeared recently in *Language Acts: Anglo-Québec Poetry, 1976 to the 21st Century* (co-edited by Swift and fellow Canadian poet, Jason Camlot) he has this to say about Robert Allen, the Canadian poet who passed away in 2006:

> The subject-matter of Robert Allen's poetry is beautifully varied. It is also variously beautiful, though not unafraid to wander into less seemly territory. Allen is a conscious voyager into undiscovered realms, able to write of a closely observed newt, cannibalism after an air disaster, the Magellanic cloud, the beauty of a North Hatley winter and Errol Flynn's cock. Everything is all here.

When poets write about the poets they profoundly admire they often end up writing about themselves. A few of the very specific details aside, everything Swift says about the work of his mentor, Robert Allen, is also true of his own. Swift's poetry is stunning in its variety. The selection from his third collection, *Rue Du Regard*, published in 2004, includes both "The Influence of Anxiety at the Seaside with Tea", his wonderfully achieved nod to that quiet high priest of lush and difficult language, Wallace Stevens, and, "Note to the Editor", his uproariously informal satire on his own adventures as a poetry editor at online magazine *Nthposition* and elsewhere.

Swift adheres to Yeats' advice: "sing whatever is well made." He is a rigorous editor, and then some, when it comes to his own poems; far harder on his own work than he would ever be on anyone else's. Paradoxically, Swift is also one of contemporary poetry's great democrats. From his early days in his native Montreal, through his time living first in Budapest, then Paris and now London, he has been a keen and incisive promoter of other people's poetry.

The Chronicle of Higher Education once compared the work he has done on behalf of others to "that of Ezra Pound's in the 10s and 20s of the last century, in Paris and London." It is high praise well deserved. Swift has been an enthusiastic promoter of the best in all kinds of poetry, from formalist to political to performance to experimental. His work as a poetry impresario has, I should say, profoundly influenced my own approach to organising poetry events here in Galway City. Without Todd Swift the poetry world would be a poorer, duller place.

The publication by Salmon Poetry of his *New and Selected Poems* is a momentous occasion because it is the first collection of Swift's poetry to be published in these Isles. It includes generous selections of work from his first four collections (first published in Montreal, Quebec by the small, innovative press DC Books, founded by Louis Dudek). Swift takes the reader on a voyage across 80 poems written between 1988 and 2008, from the early promise and energy of his superb first collection, *Budavox* (1999), to impressive new poems such as "Fertility" and "One Hundred Lines."

Todd Swift has spent enough time promoting others. It is time now for him to take the main stage himself.

KEVIN HIGGINS
Galway City, 2008

The White Kitchen

Yes, you are gone
and I believe that bodies rot
when buried in the ground,

though as to what happens
to living creatures
that walk their peripheries

in a distant town
I am helpless to say.
Not dead then, but distant.

On the occult telephone
your voice sounds
as oddly rushed as from the ether,

summoned by a crone.
I can add nothing new
to metaphysical conjecture,

I am no oiled and bound Egyptian,
have no name for what's been done
here in your absence's white kitchen.

Gun Crazy

Against the world, just us.
Behind, a trail of gas stations,
small banks, the meat packing plant,
knocked over. FBI Telexes
clatter like town gossips across America:
Barton Tare and Laurie Starr, dangerous
and armed. How did it begin?
Neon wakes me, I peel back blinds
to jackhammer rain, shake a Lucky
from the pack, and light.
Behind, on the tangled bed, you are mine,
every inch of your easy hunger, your fear
cold and material in the night.

Where are we two going? When we get
there, how will we know we've finally
arrived? Mexico, possibly, but the bills
are marked and the Feds hot on our tails.
The first time we met, I shot six matches
off the crown on your head, at a carnival,
won five hundred bucks. The moment
the matches flared, I knew my bullets
would always be true, direct. You kill
out of a necessity verging on need, I
cannot squint the eye down to that degree,
my hand trembles at the sight of flesh targets.
Still, I'll end up putting a bullet in your heart
up in the San Lorenzo Mountains, in the mist.

That first night I aimed and squeezed
I should not have missed.
You wake and call me over to the bed.
Then I'm down in your arms and kissed.
Your mouth sets off all four alarms.
How can a man be so made
from moments of early loss?
I was always gun crazy,
so good at one clear thing:
hitting what I could barely see.
I see nothing in the darkness now, only
one part moving on the bed, my body
pressed like a pistol
into the small of your cries.

Evening on Putney Avenue

When all the lawns are shutting off,
neighbours each with a porch light to close,
I stand in my driveway and smoke alone,

not allowed to smoke inside my house,
and look down Putney Avenue, left and right,
as I was taught to do before crossing,

but stay in my place, watching for the moon
to change, as people wait for green.
A boy and girl shoot past in a red car,

she turns her face, an instantaneous affair,
then it takes Mortlake. A family with another
girl slowly talks through the leaves,

acknowledging no part of me. I step back
into the lilacs, to let them go without
having to recognise my slight presence.

She also turns, her eyes see my new haircut,
but she goes on with her parents,
her skinny legs in black summer shorts.

She accompanies my mind to the end of the block.
Once, this was the street where
I played soccer-baseball, and kick-the-can.

I must know the ground here like no one else,
the way the caterpillars crawl along the arm.
I lost a lot here, and when I was gone.

I toss the cigarette off the curb and prepare
to go back in. My parents are in there, warm.
The spring air is chillier than you might expect.

For all the things I do not have, I have
this night, suburban and sublunar, to collect,
like a paperboy cast in stone.

This Was How One Lasted

I used to pretend I was a dolphin
when I swam in the lake.
I was a boy then, skin smooth
and untanned, because I read
all day on the lawn, my legs
covered by a blue towel, with a pine
tree marking my chair and book
in a high, clean shade, the light
tart needles of windblown air.
Twice in a day, only, would I
become upright, and go down
to the water, once before noon
and then again near evening.
I was thin and young, with shivers

and would wait for something
to call me in. Often I had no reason
to dive for an hour, staying there
watching the sunbathing girls
on the raft, turning slowly
along the chain that tied them
to the bottom, the gallon cans
filled with sand. Spiders, landed
like aliens on the moon of green
linoleum of that raft, made it their
ghastly headquarters, so I never
went there. Finally, I would walk in
until the line of my belly
was drawn in the lake, risen

over my startled penis, to join
the line, and descend.
I had no water eyes,
closed and forced a form
I was to plummet
straight free. This was
my extending moment—
all union and calm,
the sweep and underneath
of sensation, flight in the springs
that crossed my body,
heat and cold turned on
and off, like faucets, as I passed,
a fast and silent submarine.

Unborn, beyond exposed things,
saved in the water, I began with nothing
but hands and a lidded mind, and life
and thought through to the ocean
where I was elsewhere,
also, at the same time,
my bones a sweet bread, slid
into the mammalian sea, a knife.
I never came up on behalf of oxygen,
searched for pockets where
I stayed—my feeling was
this was how one lasted
after drowning and dead,
was better than above.

In the Future

It will be possible
To program sleep
And wake up as any object

So desired: cars,
Compacts, microwave
Ovens, VCRs, ladies'

Razors, laser discs, Ming
Vases, plastic gloves,
Vibrators, and specially designed

Sex-chairs, walking sticks,
Lipstick, a former lover.
You will be able to turn into first

One and then another of these things
At will, enjoying the inanimate
Splendour of being usable,

Reusable, as the case
Might be, knowing that
In the next chamber

Your friends or mating partner may
Already be waiting
As their own favourite instrument.

Mary Veronica Swift, 1914–1991

1.

The cosmology of a room is uneven.
It has containment and leakage the heavens
cannot hold or set, it has been lived through,
beds the weight and blood of persons
having moved, and traced, their outlines
by breath and dying. Mary Veronica Swift,
you fell in passing from your comforter,
your head abruptly struck
where the white radiator's iron coiled.

2.

I have brought away trinkets from where you died,
Christs bent into each conceivable trident of pain,
and will fit them to purposes on my Verdun wall.
Paint leaps at the hammer, cracked like ice
in the Arctic as it heaves, to both sides, broken.
Plaster flours my fingers, leavened hands
setting aside Mother and Child
to inspect the damage:
a Nile zigzags from baseboard to ceiling.

3.

Now I hang your Dublin cross,
made of fine linen,
saved behind glass in a frame
no bigger than a face;
suffer no debt or anger
but the loss of love.
Wielding a substance known as light,
I rise to strike, like Hephaestus
tempering his blow
against the pagan nail.

Ways of Counting

When next I see you see me,
You will be young, I will be thirty.

Years are like fans in plays by Oscar Wilde.
Ladies open them, part of the scenery.

In your hands shake out our days.
They beat the air, cool our faces.

Each fold, tinted variously, is a time,
And the beauty of the whole was planned.

Now I am alone, until rejoined,
When you decide to finish the book of us

Borrowed by a friend. It is body
And mind, mind and body, being so extended.

When next I feel you feel mine,
I will be like a fork given back its favourite tine.

Suitor

Brushing your eye,
it came out.
Embarrassed to have done that,
I bent quickly
to retrieve your blue object
under the skirts of the end table.

When I brought it up
to your dark place,
I found you had forgotten
you had ever seen from it,
moved your head aside, gently
so as to indicate disinterest,
as you do when you are tired
of my brushing of your hair.

Understanding very little but my duty,
I went at the other,
in a moment had you
in completed darkness.
Your head raised itself, backward, quietly,
prepared to not remember, ever,
what would be next.

Kanada Post

I remember some other life as if it's mine.
My country has become a stamp, weather,
and what my mother says, over the phone.

I miss less than expected. My small house,
the brick dust, the white slanting porch,
and the things we don't mention anymore.

Soon front yards were new others, mowing.
Schools that'd been one way, were not, now.
And the snow. It falls and builds great towers,

closing off what is within from what's without.
Snow-blowers with their dark, regurgitated slush.
Trees catch ice, become impressive with April.

My birth month is rain and light, a dancing pair
of skaters. The smell of winter breaking like glass.
I never loved the ones that deserted, and not those

that did the replacing. Neither were mine to lose.
The frail blue of early night, in late spring, shone.
It's not a country if it only happens when it's gone.

Gorazde

Men and women are small
When bullets are put inside them,
They lie down like stones.
All the bodies leaning on the ground.

Like children throwing glass at rain,
This could almost be strange new fun;
Even when you are dead, gentlemen,
No one will forget what you have done.

The Kite Flyer

knows she is in the wrong business
if escape is uppermost
in her mind: lengthens the curve
of string to tighten the wind, and drives
across winter from above, her bird
hunting after currents, folds
in sky affairs, strengthening
play and purpose in a mild force
of handiwork, the resourceful box swerving
to maintain the depth, and height
of the moon, the line. The blue
in air is rapid, achieved through steering
by sheer delight, and unbroken plans
urging spirits out of things.

January 20, 1993

What an unbelievably sad day.
I have just watched the woman I love

fly away in a plane. Meanwhile
Bill Clinton is getting his hand raised.

He'll be President of the United States
by the time she lands in Seattle.

The airport, after she passed through
the frosted doors to get her bags X-rayed,

is like an empty zoo. Space for all sorts
of absent animals. I have three miles

of corridor to myself, push invisible
luggage around. Since she went beyond

those doors I've been a porter
with no one to carry nothing for.

You could say: that man is lost.
In the lounge I raise a Bud to the stars.

Lost at Austerlitz

Water On Mars, sun at Austerlitz,
Human Genome Mapped, us lost:
driving, six hours from Budapest.

Your U-turn got us up to Slavkov
after a love-battle we now regret.
In 1805, this light sliced through

dawn mist, struck lake ice, cut off
the Hapsburg army's final retreat.
N marked the general's tent above

wavelike fields, golden, bloodless.
Enough to have been here, Napoleon
announced, to his still-living men.

Austerlitz, June 2000

The Last Days of St. Lambert

First, the houses went, their white paint
curling up over in the flames
like sheets of paper thrown from a window

caught in a wind. Nothing could be saved
but the porches, which all withstood
the blaze, as if wood from another tree,

this one of stone, had been substituted
invisibly, one morning.
Then, all the churches disappeared,

as if nothing had ever been on the lots,
the ground fallow, the soil black and good
and with a small collection: one girl—

an arrowhead; a boy—a pierced American
coin, through which his eye could see
a roaring sun, and her red hair.

The New Fedora

In Budapest gentlemen wear fedoras.
I do too, mine soft and black,
made from rabbit's fur.

Today, it nearly crossed the ring–road
sans my head, lured by the wind.
I grasped the brim

and held on with my gloved hand.
I smiled, catching my father,
being him. All the long work

of figuring manhood out, responsible
and dark, suddenly lifting
like a shy clerk just given a raise.

In My Father's Briefcase

Pink and blue file folders, as if his work
Divided into boys and girls, circa 1960,
Stacked, beside uncapped black markers,
Whose ink was gone. Acceptance letters,

Which he'd sign at the kitchen table after
A careful review—in his minute scrawl.
Maybe, also, green gum with chlorophyll
And an old *Montreal Star* sports section.

If I had asked, and he had remembered,
There might be a few *Richie Rich* comics.
Twelve pennies orphaned in the corners
Would rattle when he closed it up again.

Sheer Speculation

Do the people who don't love us
gather around our absence to laugh?
There must be such a meeting place
of the disinterested who spurned our
passionate, pleading letters—a station
in a deserted Eastern European spot
evacuated after leaked radiation, with

trains rusted on their rails, and baggage
still on the platform, where dropped.
In this dusty, abandoned setting, how
perfect their colloquium would seem,
as roses were dissected, petals savaged,
and the words we used to woo them
tacked to dingy notice boards, uselessly,

now that no passengers dawdle here—
ordered from the town by local authorities.
Or, is it likely, if our unlovers do flock,
they congregate in a more upscale venue,
above the gleaming, hard-to-get metropolis,
with a sweeping view of lower rooftops.
Or is indifference all, do they just let us go

from swan-beaks? Is there no hosting of those
who never cared one whit, or if they did, did so
too late, or rain-cancelled our world in a broken
date? If so, then where do we half-hearts reside?
Denied daydreams, exiled from reveries, we sip
at short straws, that bent, bring us no soda fizz:
truth known, ghosts of a chance that never was.

Liszt Ferenc tér

You wait an hour in the square, at the table
under the striped umbrella.
She's late: is this your next misunderstanding,

or (the part everyone hopes someone else will play)
did she step out into the arms of a tram?
Either way, your sun–burnt waiter glares,

displeased by the meagre order:
one cola, with a straw, while no one you know
arrives in high heels, laughing, loud as life.

Budapest, June 2001

The Seven Wonders of the World

The world's seven wonders are elsewhere.
But there are many more that go uncounted.
She was one, he another. We each have
our own list: scents, pleasant performances,
evenings, particular rains, the bright stacking
of fruit in a bowl, a pencil's shading, her
surprising ability to reintroduce a sense

into a forgotten place. The centuries
will have much else to say, to add. I
cannot astonish anyone who has not been
here themselves—within the pyramid,
the hanging gardens, under the stars, flowers
of balanced stonework and light—seeing
portioned marble, feeling curved bodies,

handling a sin; cradling a son or daughter.
The layers of descent through time's sensations
are appalling to enumerate, all the wonderful
things, apart from the dreadful, we may
have, or chance to behold, to obtain
through any of the senses that remain prepared:
her hands with their slender fingers, her diamond's

very, very small inclusions choreographing light,
and the parrots and the monsoons, and almonds
and tanning butter spread across bronzed skin,
and the salt of the water, and the ice
cut into clarity under the loupe of the moon;
not ever ideal, for too real, but for all that,
worthy of any ancient worship you might devise—

or for that matter, a leopard's eyes, a violet swan.
We could go on and on, and yet we won't.
How to bother with sensuous excess, when it is
all around, and always present, like omniscience
is said to be, except this concerns pleasure,
the fulfilling absolutes that exceed our potential,
as if we had cupped our hands under a waterfall

having expected the barest minimum of a dribble,
and been inundated with a torrential satisfaction.
How can we desire when we are sensual Pharaohs
with all the gems and servants of the senses
spread before our wonder, as if arisen in a tomb,
our cats and many mistresses and rubies spilling
from out of their comfortable waiting stations?

After the End of the World

After the end of the world
there is much work to be done:
laying on of hands, readings
from *The Book of Alternate Prayer,*
burying, burying the dead everywhere.

And gift-giving. I, for one,
brought you a garnet necklace
and a protractor set,
both things you said
you had always wanted.

For a week we had sex in a building
we could never have afforded
the rent for, before the Terrible Event.
It was not the loss of our parents,
not the blackout of Cable News,
that made us blue.

Remember, we grew up with Doomsday
like an invisible friend:
not quite believed in, but always there.
Disappointed would hardly be
the right word to use.

No, it was not murderous instrumentality
that did our life away.
After all we had planned, suddenly
it was you, who quickly cried, then went on
like a thief without warning,
into the Southern Wasteland,
while I stayed behind,
applying gauze bandages until morning.

Last Year's Model

What happened on the forest floor
is old, forgotten, a short story.
Moss covers her mouth, many months

branch over soft rot, stale metamorphosis.
Very few identifying marks remain
with the rain and feeders having come in,

a face masked with bark and mushroom.
The breastbone picked clean, steam
is evident from humus and flesh

in the ageing litter of darkness around
the scuttling beetles in the abandoned park.
No one addresses this unfashionable

woman, worn to the bone, sporting
a lipstick of soil, eyeshadow of root,
her chin beneath a toadstool's pout.

My Name Is Panama

The Pacific is ultramarine,
pelicans stamped on
the envelope of air,

mailing themselves over
the Canal Zone, narrow
girdle of a toucan-mad isthmus.

I enter the Hotel Central.
The rooms have a stained-sheet
feel, rented at a desk longer

than some lives, low,
holding seven drained bottles
of Canada Dry.

My Panama hat high on Bolívar,
I am ready—*sin nombre*—
to set sail for San Fran, or Shanghai.

Panama City, 1999

Hume Knoll

The trees on Hume knoll have grown
since the highway cut down ones
they replaced, a hundred yards on,
no longer smaller than any of us.

When workers come to widen the route
they won't know they're walking where
Melita and her husband Ian took care
to block diesel-torn wind with firs.

None of the woodcutters will recall
that fifty years ago this was a bare hill—
snow-rounded—crossed with daffodils—
now another year raised in ice—

but as stiff green guards fall around
the cutters will recover older ground—
finding, during work's pause, grass
my grandparents mowed—as it was.

Water, Running

Our marriage is water running
in a bathtub with no plug.

For a moment, I want to disagree,
then don't, impressed by the image:

your image, for what is, after all
only you and me. Or, me and not

enough of you. But then, language
doesn't always connect so truly

to somewhere else: fall over and across
another thing just so, neatly joining

worlds together, like difficult puzzles
working out suddenly, from new-angled

words and other meanings piling on—
like those many-layered fountains

you loved, at the gardens in Istanbul,
which in their motion are symbols of

an Islamic paradise in letterless
signs more pure than if written;

like cold champagne cascading
over wide glasses at a wedding.

The More Deserved

We know nothing better than what
we never get to call our own, space
it should be filling, its masterful lack.
We marry our unachievements, make

resentment a second home: a garden
we keep out back, for little pleasures.
Her ring slipped off a finger, the line
slack now at the bottom of the ravine,

promotions passing overhead like jets:
the day we least deserve grand failure,
we will receive it at the door, delivered
by gloved hand, tipping for a telegram.

The Usher

We're taken to our seat,
the feature already on,
by a girl or boy of sixteen
with a flashlight,

upsetting someone, pushing
darkness to where we sit.
I do not pretend to know
how it is we keep

so silent here, though
screeching with the knife
shining its fresh droplets,
sutured into the nightmare:

a face, my beloved, not in a next,
the same world, but apart.
Sorrow flickers, light-traced,
names flowing up a screen.

If only the girl or boy (in
costume, with a bow-tie)
were leading us to a balcony
to have our first kiss,

I could hug these images
into me, a pillow of nostalgia:
my parents, travelling by
the kind of plane with propellers

over an itinerary of yellow seas,
missing, but in the absence filled
golden with a kid's love
of mysterious passages.

A child's bed is a narrow
strip to land a history of regret,
its endless map of deserts
and spent pavilions,

all monkey grins gone to bone.
No movieland, no glittering trope—
all icons cascading out of hand—
available to me now, who sees

a swaybacked usher lean nearby,
prepared, gum cracking, to lead
me, through doors with portholes
swinging, like in a busy kitchen.

So if I turn I will see nothing.
Nothing to see. Except what is seen
now, before the visuals go.
I want to see you, see you so.

Usher, lead me with your torch
into the purple caravan
of rippling dreams, to the porch
where antebellum maidens

sing, where French foreign
devils turn the foes, where
nicotine is sinful as a pear,
and with its sinuous nectar

grey-glows; usher me beyond
cuttings, technique, daily
reels, all the human scenes.
The light's gone out of this.

That Girl In Autumn

It always happens to me in the autumn:
I'm out twirling an umbrella on Fifth Avenue—
the full fetching gamine-paradigm—
the svelte feisty happy hour ingénue—
the fresh delirious elegant coquette
tom-boyish, crazily slender who, not shy, slinks
yet leaps as she breezy and feline, feral
yet easy, though never, as a rule, ever
that sleazy—parades her reflection
down the cool, brisk and gritty canyons.
That's the kind of girl I, day-tripping, fanciful,
sort of become—or imagine getting to be—
dizzy and well-gloved in Hart Crane's Manhattan,
date-eligible: a sassy New Critic of British *Vogue*.

Perfume and New Shoes

The sun just flown in for Cannes,
Protected by bullet-proof Ray-Bans

She poses at the microphone, saying
Hip, bitchy things about Americans,

Claims she's never met a book
She'd be caught in bed reading,

Confesses to having liked fellating
The latest settler-colony sensation

To have socked his way onto screen via
Stubble, six-pack habit, the connections.

It's that kind of day: over-the-top
Glamour sashaying past bellhops

Right up to the desk, getting a look;
And all I have on my jaunty agenda

Under blue May skies in designer Paris
Is a note to buy perfume and new shoes

So that I can walk down the red carpet,
To stand beside you and say I really do.

The Influence of Anxiety at the Seaside with Tea

She saw the beauty of the sea and could not rival it
For lack of depth, for cut and clarity. It screened
Itself like a blue movie. It was a mandolin. Flat,
And on a continuous feed. The sea was a pool

On a spool, a fluid, wet circuitry, a freakish
Cola, without sugar or fizz. The sea was in business
To sell waves to sand; to deliver cetaceans to nets;
The sea is a grey-green, moon-led elephant

Who always forgets. She sank into the Sargasso
Of herself, and touched a wreck. It yielded doubloons
And Maltese falcons and other encrusted valuables;
She scooped the ice-cream starfish and the jelly

Of the sperm whales, and the cardboard villainy
Of certain sharks. She slid like a shadow, a dagger
Of slim ease in a pressurised medium. She sang
Oxygen and filtered sunlight, and salty tunes.

She was overcome by *Harmonium*; flush poems
With quince and tea and royal-rococo references
To the world and imagination; dove, in homage;
She wrapped herself in a peacock-daubed kimono

In silken envy. How could she not be immensely
Injured by the creations of Florida and San Juan?
The ocean and its sisters set out its store of baubles,
And she bought them. She was the eye and womb

Of the stanzas that melted and ran through the town
Like rough blue-white bulls storming a seawall.
This was the first performance of the storm, the horn
Section was off. The rain pulled toads from its hat.

The world was brushed with cream like a scone.
Happiness was inherited and could not be taxed.
She swam Olympic strokes, and sang circular tracks.
The sea undressed, a Parisian girl, *oh la la, mais oui.*

Monsieur Pigeon's Best Machine

I would like my cemetery to be shaped
like the one at Montparnasse, bordered
by Rue Froidevaux, Boulevard
Edgar-Quinet, Raspail, and

on the fourth side, lit apartments
whose small square windows look out
on the graves of Aron, Bainville,
Belmondo, and Cortazar.

Autumn makes sorrow smell good,
gives one an appetite to go after tombs.
They fill me with comfort, because, after
so long, they are still here: the names

kept (Sartre, Man Ray), and the low, flat
trays left out, to put small gifts on, as if
thanking the dead for their hospitality.
Speaking of which, my favourite tombstone

belongs not to an industrialist or chess
champion (though they are here in numbers),
not even to the Mexican President Porfirio
Díaz, but instead to a homely inventor:

Charles Pigeon. His grave is topped
with the most grotesque figure of sentiment.
We come to his last resting place
beside his wife. It is a large, green bed

(the air did that) and in it, there they both are:
he doodling new mechanisms in a notebook,
completely dressed, down to the detail of
a pocket watch and vest; she, more relaxed,

is turned slightly aside, one hand put out
to his thigh, as if to say: *Charles, let's make
whoopee.* This scene of married life
is Monsieur Pigeon's best machine:

one which carries all who pass by it,
immediately, from our poor century
back to his, when such contentment,
between man and wife, was a basic right.

At any rate, he thought so, and put it up
(in the path of revolution and economies)
to cap their night with a fixed ornament,
reinventing tenderness as a monument.

The Great Rose Windows

aisles of flung light, adroit colour: sliding with the eye,
spacious, complete,
by high points built, to foster air—

posturing, brightest of truth's many accents, newly spoken,
in glass, urine, lead—so here,
roseate universals, bold blueness,

approximate the full depth of God—a blueness Neptune
could not bear—lung-breaking blueness,
Chartres-named, these

blue upright punctuations,
light-winded, shunting sun,
burst fecund images, through, back, into dark, to bloom—

flowers burying bright heads underground—
sight's inversion,
soul-symbol—this casting inwards through illumination,

from mannered stone to fluidity:
vision, constant in inconsistency:
blood-reds also,

field-yielding fire-green, taking your whole sight up to surprise,
shining in intensities crafted, stained.
The sheer drapery of light!

Now darkness tailoring shade folds
to rim and run in glazier's vinegar
details: copper, oxides, known here, fuse

in a kiln, master each jigged panel set in H, crosses of cobalt,
ruby, yellow sulphur-root, a table
chalky, delightful, a best-seen cluster, rebuilt cloisters,

stone-taken lightly,
armatures mounted, light's fruit ripe, ready—renovated—
in the life-like aisles.

Homage To Charlotte Rampling

Not to be just a "skinny sado-masochist"
twisted past all recognition, suspenders
over fishbone torso and tweenie nipples
singing in the death camp to your lover:

that was, Charlotte, a wise career move.
So was the departure to alter ego Paris.
Marriage suited you better than nakedness
set in the most perverse circumstances

imaginable. Older, in *Under The Sand*,
Ozon's film, your eyes identify the body
of your drowned husband, no longer human
but swollen by the sea, putrid and sexless.

Your gaze lies over the available absence
we all tend to as volatile organic creatures.
The loss and horror and the contamination
under the white dry sheets in the mortuary,

pulled aside like the skin from a surgical
wound. Your eyes hover, they stay open.
We see you struggle, there, in that moment with
what we all have to face. Your face dies for us.

Leaving Paris

So now I bid farewell to my barber
Hugues Renaut, who I saw
For two years in Paris, every six weeks,
For Coiffure & Soins. This last

Of my times with him, Hugues sits
In his own chair, the one I was always in,
As his brother works his thinning skull.
He gazes into the mirror like a king

Whose crown has come off his head.
Then they switch places, twins at home
Sharing brush, comb, and scissors.
Although I promise to return long before

My black hair has reached my collar,
We both know the distances we won't
Cross to come across each other again.
His usual banter pared down to lack,

I shake hands and step out into rue d'Assas.
The lady at the Tabac sold Marlboro Lights
And English papers to me. Nothing more.
But, after only a year or so, I loved her,

Even when she stood behind the counter
Beside her husband, a hulking man
With a trimmed beard and no smile.
One of her hands was missing a finger.

Mr. Lent

I'm Mr. Lent, what's burnt
Is bent, and put back in place.
Slap me, and expect a smack
Of gentleness. I scissor

Motley and cut out loss.
The paperwork is eschewed.
I sleep in the air, and wrap
Up in asphalt. Nothing is

The Lord's fault, unless
You want to blame love
For dizzy-footed blathering.
Every piece of cloth

She coats me in is stolen fox.
Watch me dilly-dally
With the Bank of England's
Locks. Military brandishings

Are timely and will disappear.
I am Mr. Lent, give up
Success and Equitable Poise.
Your houses will inherit sand.

You scoop and bruit,
And get down to mashing.
I am waiting wearing bells
And will Shim Sham with thee.

Marylebone

So, I had a fight with the Frenchman
Who smashed our crystal wedding present
Against the side of his moving van.
He'd taken exception to the small size
Of the English windows, narrow stairs.
We'd debated the merits of his abandoning

Eighty-six boxes of personal belongings
To the British weather, much in evidence.
He looked the sort to snap near children,
Then write memoirs in Genet's old prison.
His shaved head raised the hairs on mine
For how he'd self-barbered it, done free,
Discounting the odd supergrass cicatrice.

The landlord's henchman, his Union
Jack hung up next door for all to see
(With the Internet surveillance camera
Connexion) lounged in a biker jacket
That Gunn might've taken out on loan
From Brando, and quipped *that action*
Was like pissing over yer young bride.

Cross-channel tensions weren't eased
By this observation: urbane as Niven.
Saw him and his cronies off with London
Pride in a pub at our corner. Walked on
And came across a plaque marking
The name of A.J. Ayer; who'd died there.

A Ceremony of Carols at Cripplegate

In low pews, Anglican or just off-the-street,
How still they sit, to listen to the air become
Music: high seriousness snakes

Through space, and flicks each elderly ear,
Swollen, becalmed by hair. The old women, too,
Have swallowed a third beauty, after childhood

And childbirth. How venal, then,
To notice all the time-worn suits,
The dresses far past their fashion.

Decrepitude cradles us. It was ancient men
Who surrounded the babe as he emerged,
Peering from sand-blind eyes

To stare at holiness. As if it might cure
Their own worried flesh.
There's no rose as virtuous or fair as Christ

But when he rises will those who came before
Do so as well? If not this may be the last world
In which I share a carol

With so many bleary souls, coughing
At the wine-fed interval. Is it worth such pain,
This short intermission of great upward sound,

To break the loam to creep among dusk again?
We should thank Christ there is no return.
We go from wholesome aficionados of Anon

To a thing awful; with its brains, pluck and rhythm
Turned and wormed like some
Discarded instrument devoid of all five strings.

Anton Bruckner Choir
St. Giles Cripplegate, 18 December 2003

Ballad of the Solitary Diner

When I eat alone, I am alone.
Thank God I have my books.
Friends? Not many.
My wife, in her tower, earning money.
A few who live in other countries

Too far to go to share a meal.
When I sit down at noon I often feel
As sad as a man having married
The moon. You cannot love well
Someone you can't share a spoon

With, be it soup or salad.
The waiter or waitress assumes
The identity of a temporary friend,
But they are busy with their errands
And soon go to other people.

Then, as my tea cools, and the day
Gets weak in the head and fails
To keep appearances up,
I put on my winter coat to pay,
Leave a pound for their trouble,

And go out the way I came in.
Thank God I have my books.
I can tell by the limited smiles
As I turn, I no longer have my looks.
It is a shame we have to eat at all,

It hurts us to have to be so open
And quiet, even as we appear social.
If I could get by on my poetry
I'd eat a page a day in my flat.
I'd stay thin, and not become fat

As all this dining out in the world
Has made me: yes, and with nothing
To show for the tedious work
Of getting it down, but one more check
And a dark walk home, through a town.

Note to the Editor

Thank you for your interest in my work,
which means a lot to me
and my seven brothers,
who live near you,

and are karate experts.
Don't be shy to tell me what you think.
Praise Jesus!
And thank you once again.

This is the only anthology
I have been asked to submit to.
Submit is such a funny word, isn't it?
I hope the poems on the death of tubercular infants

do not offend you.
My sisters had this disease
and it is based on actual experience
recollected in tranquillity

but you know how that goes.
Thank you again and send me a reply
in six to seven hours
so I can tell the people I live with

all about it.
I hope I won't have to put
my disappointment hat
on today.

To My Wife Of Ninety Days

Last days involve us,
What you most resemble is
Time: its strong line, humour
And never stopping, how gentle
At once but more complicated than
That too. We first danced to become
Closer, and then again you removed fur
Coats and assumed the position of top dog.
Between the shivers of laughter, long flowers,
Drama nous and such tense beauty—so closely
Guarded and yet often released, as offset sunlight
In autumn seems poised to give, in restraint, much.
Best love, smarter, smarting, you take us past accident,
Airports and oceans, above the clouds, arguing certainty.

Whiplash in Paris

I live in the street where Huysmans died.
I should like to make something of that.
A series of poems; perhaps a novella.

J.K. Huysmans, who wrote *Against Nature*
Was an unconventional fellow.
It appears he made Proust seem robust,

The constraints of the author of *Locus Solus* less than loco.
Oscar Wilde, who also went to heaven in Paris,
Took inspiration from this.

These days our street has less to do with Yellow Books,
More with boot polish and high heels: rue Saint Placide
Is called "Shoe Street" for its many

Stores. There are also baby shops
(Which specialize in pint-sized parasols) and a sushi bar.
The street includes three young trees.

I imagine M. Huysmans was never shaded by them,
Just as I never had the pleasure to greet him
With a friendly *bonjour*. (There were good days

And bad days then, as now.)
This Monday I received a blow from behind, in a taxi,
And am in considerable pain.

I went to the American Hospital in Paris for x-rays.
The machine hollowed out my secret bone marrow
In its modern key of radiation: *voyeur; voleur:*

Reversed brother of no skin: you read me outside in.
(Madame Curie was the first
Woman in the Pantheon.)

My neck, like some exotic African princess, is circled
By a soft brace, elongating me.
Semi-agonized, I stroll down a book-irradiated street.

Cinéma du Look

Looking isn't love,
but it also pays attention.

The deliberate openness
with which blinds are left

apart, curtains wide, lights on
at all hours of the day and night.

And I, who must
work for a living, bear witness

to her changes, the shifts in
scenery, the *Cinémathèque*

française of her bedroom:
black and red lingerie, braless

t-shirt hours; the choosing
of a skirt or dress.

The Tenant of Wildfell Hall

I miss being a kid, but barely recall those parts
About chores, not getting kissed, or being ugly.
And the palpability of novels. Opening
The copy she lent that Sunday afternoon,
By Monday I was hooked, on gothic winds
And girls in cloaks, and love, for characters
That were actually her, or so I felt. Returning
The loan, she looked at me, as if I was already
Forgotten, but didn't bother to ask me not to stay.
Death's not about going to the block for a woman
Whose better husband you robustly replace.
Living is more like falling forward on your face,
Onto a scuffed parquet floor, lightly dusted
With all those who have been swept off it before.

Tomsk

"...the Siberian Athens, known for its lacy wooden buildings, furs, gold, and universities."
—Local Tourist Guide

What are lacy buildings? Was there ever
a cold Socrates, a Parthenon gilded in ice?
What long poetry, what Pythagorean tears
scattered in these bitter white winds?
What polar bears bit at what rinds?
Did Plato and Aristotle, pulled by a team
of snow-caped malamutes, decamp in Tomsk
to envision gold-smeared Greece
reborn in a frozen swamp, newly lit
by Diogenes' lamp? Did they flame
the chill-gnawed Siberian landscape
with images of icons and geometry?

What exists love says should be:
a dolphin-grey, a book-kissed, city.

Emperor

(after *Solntse*, directed by Aleksandr Sokurov)

I.

I, Hirohito, among strewn boxes
and a fractured aquarium, compose
a poem based on a cherry blossom

and a dissected crab's revealed softness
as purebred goldfish on the lab's floor
strain for filtered water, "Sea in a Glass."

The Imperial lab floods with sunlight,
burning the eyes of rare porcupine fish
pried from their reefs for my further study.

Is it snow, or hot ash, progressing calmly
outside my blinded window, placing fire
on the flayed skin of this season's face?

I was a God in fancy human dress,
selected a fine top hat from London.
Forgetting my station, not minding where

I step, or what is stepped on beneath me
(a white, scuttling spider crab maybe)—
MacArthur floating on Tokyo Bay

I removed my divinity like a glove;
petals away from a Chrysanthemum Throne.
The cold instruments of surrender signed—

a document to be skinned of whatever
fabric mere holiness is made up from,
I now stand before my smallest mirror

to observe ordinary nakedness.
Here is my entirely mortal hand
that may close upon a sea urchin's spines

to suffer the same pins and needles as
any human in the land. No longer
will trembling men button up linen shirts

or kneel in my bunker to explain how
a superior force borrowed the sun,
laying waste to our ancient paper towns.

2.

Today feels as much like winter as when
my father, Emperor before me, seeing
Northern Lights, impossible above Tokyo,

summoned me through four ministers
to speak of the sky's bright coruscations.
I have had to endure the long time

in which my wife and children lived
as if I were destroyed, under bombardment—
knowing their mourning as my own.

I missed the appointed afternoons,
when advisors would escort them to me,
so that I might present them long letters,

or read aloud from a masterful composition;
amateur of all, polyglot, ichthyologist,
I know the hours divided against us alleviate

our souls, make us speak new ways.
The sea forever inspires meditation
in peacemaker and noble warrior alike.

I measured my divinity in ocean-study,
so as to know, like common people who adore
the great ruler floating far above them,

each pulsing complexity under
the surface of alarmed, tentative waves
that always tremble like an organism

shocked or rattled by a sudden change.
I have looked at photographs of film stars also,
and felt great sadness for all living things

that move, to experience the minutiae of the day,
in a rock pool, which a greater eye envisions.
This much I learned from marine biology:

each way we mourn or find a motion
is determined by a higher instrumentality;
as if all creatures were forever in a bomber's sights.

Our bodies are examined by light's callipers, then
let drop, as if caught for momentary pleasure,
into the sea, which abandons, recalls, lifts and is.

Gentlemen of Nerve

I have become my neighbour or the author or the man
I saw in the photo, when I was thirteen; I've slipped in
To his life, the one where you get to be the has-been

Movie writer; get to be the fellow who adores his wife;
The forty-year-old who walks slowly down boulevards
In springtime, thinking of nothing much, sidling along

With a mumble, instead of a song, in his punctured heart;
Now I know what they were doing when they were
Doing it; not exactly, for that was their lot, then; but well

Enough to hum the approximate ontology they unknit.
I have slipped in to the opening along their side,
Entered the weave of their nearby manhood, to coincide

With the shyness of a gentle soul who holds out
For some other day, some boon, a grand foretold
Coming in to confidence (and confidences); a Chump

At Oxford in a silk-lined coat who'd jump a fence
To avoid a bullying leaf or an unkind glance; a gentleman
Gentled by nothing so much as having sort of grown old

Without having ever advanced, in terms of career,
In terms of science, beyond the fields of expectant fear
That the sweet girl who holds him tight might evaporate

And all his books, thoughts and friends will disappear
Like stars, which look quite risky in the sky. So if
I am this guy, where is he now, past having had his own

Slippage moment, when he came into his three-piece Geist?
He might have driven far, stopped at the coast, for a well-
Earned cigar, maestro of leaning knowingly into a sea breeze;

For, the exact moment I turned forty and had insight into him
He was set free, to flow or saunter at unidentified ease, no
Longer a person observed or wondered at, but a ghostly skim

Of atoms, then other particles wafting to some inexact home,
As a genie exceeds the prison house of his wishes, to fly late
But gladly beyond the bottle's stoppered rim; so now I hesitate,

Poised, a diver on the doorframe of my impressionable bungalow,
My blissful villa, my flat, my porch, my mansion, my estate—
Until some kid spies me out as curious, unimaginably aged, so

When their grey stubble hits the marker they'll zap to my face,
Slip in to my statehood, reassemble a mixed-blessings-self or two,
While, sweet as rain after drought, I dance out and over as I go.

I'm in Love with a German Film Star

Somewhere in Kansas or wherever Wichita is,
I stop to dally with a waitress in a summer dress

under a diner's neon kiss; I wear a UPS
uniform, drive for them. The name tag lies

when it says: G.W. Pabst. I make a highway
angel by slyly helicoptering sleeved arms

on the line that divides the independent cinema
of this scene. I have the ball cap and the smirk,

am filled with an unbearable urge to be always
thirty-two and to marry a girl named Miss Miss.

I'm filled with the luminous possibilities
of American landscape as it unfolds in movies.

If I was a plane I'd never have to land—
I'd be the land, you see, I'd already be the land

and the way wings spread over and below,
the way a shirt is also a stain is also a shadow.

Tokyo Elevator Girl

Ginza elevator girl—your sliding white gloves
operating doors offer a flowing constraint
trained to describe departments

in gestures shy yet free: the gifted stroke
you impress upon monotony makes
any floating creator envy your

miniaturized way: a slim balance,
uniformed perfection, a glide in control's
direction, art's stays. Your command

of this lifting cubicle with its set-piece play,
classically ruled to unfold in one time and place,
delights me. I'd rise with your levels for hours,

honouring this quiet mastery, or
go to the ground floor where antique clocks
are displayed, under the granite facade.

Modest Proposal

Every word counts, he said.
   And then he counted them.
      I saw my mother's dress.

It was in a garden and she brought
   Out a tossed salad, laid
      The plate on my lap as I read

William Carlos Williams;
   May; my body sixteen.
      How old was she? Thirty-seven

Or thereabouts. The tomatoes
   Were lovingly sliced.
      His look returned me to this.

If it is poetry, no need to ask,
   He added. Use your fingers
      As when you comb your hair

Before going in to see the one
   You will ask to marry, mirrored
      In the hall, the clock a heart

And the words throat-clotted,
   The tie poorly handled. There.
      How many words for the task?

Not the number, the distance.
   The sum of how to rightly say
      Hope under pressure's light.

It isn't what you write down
      That carries the full weight;
            It's what they heard, and why.

And so I went in and was shy
      And turned my phrases. She
            Told me to go to blazes.

I turned, when she held on and on.
      The altar vow has only so many words
            For how darkness binds, goes bright.

Brando

You weren't Stella, I wasn't Stanley.
We never had the heat or the bare bulb
coloured with a hood, didn't ever
quarrel nights over Napoleon's code,
law's cheap dividends. I never wore
a t-shirt, oiled in sweat, a Polack god
swaggering from sex, bourbon and pride.
You never made it up with me after,
your angel wings stuck back on with string.

We never aroused the neighbours
or lost ourselves breaking out of life
via love-making's bending of the bars;
we never got that escape from Sing Sing.
I never boxed your sister into a corner
or tore her manners to tatters, a cat
adept with claws that catch the tin and slide.
We could elide the one thing and the other
but we never taught ourselves that play

or took that kind of New Orleans ride.
We couldn't outdo Brando, barely tried.
I once asked you to consider my ring.
You let me kiss you once or twice, hung up
the phone. Marlon, I hope, would've shown up
at your door, and let it be known he was
not to be denied, expressing madness in his method,
acting full-grown, wild. He'd have won you,
I'd wager. His strut, his form, his danger

and blown-out grace; he had an emperor's
face; was gross and beautiful in one
corpulent bet with a body's two-sided
coin. A genius, then, at being Janus.
Had he aimed for my teen dream-girl, would've
conquered her in drama class on day one
when we had to pair off, to read the parts
that broke us: I in my heart, you with other men.
I never shook off Kowalski's under-stain

pitting his shadow as he stalked, a panther
in a hot tenement cage; and you, Du Bois
or her sibling, doubled with rage, that such
a male was, at your stage, just so much raw
fiction. If only we'd been more brutal
to our fantasies, less controlled in
our diction, we might have howled out sex
to each other across the long dark summer
spaces, become passion's moving stars.

Woman at a Station

I see you off, as a woman at a station
her soldier, to the wars, unafraid of battalions
that smoke and whistle from windows as she

holds and holds, before releasing all his body,
his skin, scent, flesh, defined in the uniform;
the train goes, bearing away the adorations of

what was their joined ecstasy, unmarried love,
its little strategies of gin, fags, lamp-lit roses,
hugs and laughter in the park, the rained on rows

to which one returns, not alone with memory;
how the damp bed bears the impress of longing,
how long fingers know the mysteries of absence,

how the body lingers upon its own part in this.
To be a monk is not more or less than such as her;
the cramped travails are the same, the slow dust

gathering a dress of daily orders, flinging it on
one's shoulders in a sort of gay ritual, renouncing
hurt, or what hurt forgets to be, in all the flirting

and folly of the painted evenings, full of colour
and sad substance, the little that represents the all;
his lips and his heat are never against her, but on

her side; she reads the printed bulletins, knows
each manoeuvre as if the application of mascara
on to her own face; sees him fighting in a mirror;

is present in her mind on the field of confusion,
the battle is carried in her carriage, her motion.
So it is I see you off (my God) but cannot abandon

(even as I seek the immaterial spaces without sin
or longing) desire for you, for your attacked,
attacking body. How I aim to forget the cross

in favour of bled-out meditation, fragrant loss.
I hope you shall not return to take me up again
in your pinned arms, whirling me on a platform.

Rainbow in Blackrock

You and I were pleased
to see both ends of it

grounded, somewhere far off
and to have the colours

so delineated, the arc bright
as yolk, as blood, as a fern.

We would have accepted
such a firm, full curve

spanning the bay's entirety
as our godsend for the week

so then, consider our pleasure
at this fainter one, sistering

its brighter other in the clever sky.
To see them both cupping the blue,

in sun and rain, was proof that sea
to land elide one light enjambment.

My Universities

Debating the relative merits of Orchestral Manoeuvres in the Dark,
Or Tears For Fears, while April ice melts slowly in Westmount Park
Now appears to be less world-shaking than when, Misha G., we both
Could be smartly vehement about Richard Rorty, Boy George, Truth,
Logic & being spanked by Marianopolis twins known to us as Ruth.
Not that we were L. Cohen's heirs, but rather a pair of young pioneers
Gazing into the Future with our smoking jackets for uniforms, sayers
Of sooth but more often faux-decadent imbibers of lascivious perfumes,
Who often drank tea (before it was Pennyroyal) on mornings as Winter
Dripped away as surely as Youth does—as children crushed on looms;
If such industrial imagery seems a tad stark, consider the Reagan Years
Were also ours in Montreal; we danced: slim Japanese New Wavers,
The Cure & The Smiths, if not allies, our aural neighbours; felt Time's
Axis turn as early Eloquence (our praxis) dried up in Age's Summer.

Communal Garden

May takes hold of summer's handlebars and wobbles on.

The Call

The call, when it came
Was Hong Kong quality:
Could have been from
The next room; which it was.
I wasn't glad to take it
But the phone rang and rang
And in reverse. The voice
Kept saying cockles–mussels.
I went and took the call
And now and now
We're gathered here, that is all.

Onset

Everything's changed that once was the same:
the sun that kept its golden hair combed

has grown dirty locks; the long sunlit sky,
blue as the sea, has turned off-milk like an eye

broken in battle. The clouds bruised by
winter storms are grey. The wild birds,

lofty as gods, have taken flight from us.
The wind, once leonine, has fattened

on its legend, and lies around. The stream
which used to rustle like Sylvan leaves

now slouches with mud in its mouth, far
from its youth and eloquence. How I wish

I had been born in a time before time, when
none of these natural, beautiful things

could be taken from me. All is memory
that once was rushing full aflame.

The Trees of Saint-Lambert

are having a field day
in the minds of my mother
and father, who live there

and open their window
to autumn, like a camera
working in light's favour.

Mother, Father, please come over.
No, stay. I will come to you.
No harm done, no harm. Father,

I forgive, give me your arm. Mother,
I know and understand.
Your other hand.

The Last Blizzard

My mother showed me
the house she'd lived in
fifty years ago

when she was a girl
who threw glass
at her enemies

with a pig named Margaret.
My father kept his eyes
on the deteriorating conditions

ahead, saying: soon we won't see
a thing in front of us.
For now, we could.

The town my mother
no longer lived in
had big wood homes

with long, wide porches.
Fir trees stood nearby.
Christmas lights. At the end

of her street the river was met
by a green bridge.
As we crossed we saw icy water.

My mother pointed out
a view that had once been
on our two-dollar bill, before

counterfeiters forced them
to use a more intricate design.
She showed me her school,

where she had walked and run,
then where she moved to later on.
So what if the weather made us slow?

We stopped to watch
a white deer standing
in a white field, not moving.

The Mountain Lion

(i.m. Ian Hume)

We thought of winter
    when we saw the lion.
        Down from the mountains,
    no prey,
he made the impossible sudden

in snowfall.
    As close as, say,
        that tree.
    Still, very much a part
of each instant going.

While defining speed
    for us, our hearts, slowing,
        became the ice
    we'd raced on.
Such is vision's mystery.

It puts beauty deep
    into winter's chill.
        Fast as breath saying itself,
    he was gone:
a lithe accident,

meaty flood, rusted-gold;
    a fur-wreathed kingdom
        on the rangy slope;
    a mouth of stars
at earth-level.

The Man Who Killed Houdini

My father, when alive,
Loved to suck his stomach
In, and urge us
To ball a fist and strike
A blow, straight
To his solar plexus

Erect as Houdini should've
Been, but in the story
Never was. I'd put
My small hand softly
Against his strong flat
Gut, and push, afraid

To lay him low,
To kill him like the great
Houdini—so well did he
Describe the murder-jab
To me. And he'd fall down
Then rise in laughter.

Hydra

I did not know my own good breathing yet,
Waited on the land while you swam out far.
Rhythm cuts to feel the Hydra teething.
A heart's withholding ache is a line fear.
Voice trips the force after the stutter but
I halt to extend, to give, to utter
As a lover on the brink of water
Ponders the leaping pool where sunlight lies.
Sun's all surface where rocks break beneath
And many are the divers who have died
Joining their form with the forms below,
Hot to imply their safety was fluid—
Their falling lines a force to fly and flow.
Seething to be I sense my mind in blood.

The Oil and Gas University

The sectors interface. In Novosibirsk
She wears a hooded parka. She
Challenges outmoded ideas. She
Transforms the education–research

Manifold and provides new incentives.
She pulls her hood back to reveal
That beauty achieves real excellence
In a real–world setting. Her lips

Hit each of the seven key targets
Set by the national institute last year.
Ownership and exploitation
Have no place in this exciting dynamic.

Opportunity, however, is vital here
In this oil and gas region near the pole.
She walks past the infrastructure.
The gas flares in the fields, the tundra

Reciprocates under the white solar
Glare—then continuous darkness
Of course will eventually supplant this
Brilliant feat. High technology

Must provide a nexus and intensive
Inventories. She is beautiful and I
Wish to introduce myself to her
At the Oil and Gas University.

Taking Tea with Charles Bernstein

Lapsang Souchong with a lapsed sous chef;
Charles enjoys its smoky aroma and tarry taste.
Keemun with a Communard;
Charles delights in a lightly-scented nutty flavour.
Yunnan with a U-turning UN man;
Charles likes the maltiness with milk.
Gunpowder with Guy Fawkes;
Charles notes the soft honey taste, the little bang of it.
Chun Mee with Connie Chung;
Charles raises his eyebrows at its smoothness.
Oolong with Long John Silver;
Charles eschews milk and sugar, not wanting them to dominate.
Ti Kwan Yin with a typist quite intuitive;
Charles swoons at the fragrant infusion.
Pouchong with Pol Pot;
Charles is suspicious of the very sweet, stylish taste.
Pai Mu Tan Imperial with a pretty tanned empress;
Charles notes the small buds of this rare, white tea.
Yin Zhen with L. Cohen;
Charles spits out the silvery needles.
Jasmine with a Jass band;
Charles sits in with Bix and finds delicate modern time.
Rose Congou with a Belgian from the Congo;
Charles admires the great skill used in the handling of the leaves.
Earl Grey with Duke Ellington;
Charles considers this mandarin blend a tad traditional.
Darjeeling with Jar Jar Binks;
Charles celebrates with the "Champagne of Teas".
Dimbula with Dmitri Shostakovich;
Charles sips the light, bright, crisp tea; his mouth feels fresh.
English Breakfast with Edie Sedgwick;
Charles likes this strong bed tea.
Afternoon Tea with Anthony Blunt;

Charles bites into a cucumber sandwich.
House Blend with Olivia Hussey;
Charles is comforted by the type most people use at home.
Bubble Tea with Bazooka Joe;
Charles is amused by this beverage with tapioca balls.
Iced Tea with Richard Blechynden;
Charles, hot by now, is refreshed by this ice cold drink.

Warming

Each day, the glacier at the pole of my walk
To the store where I buy stamps and milk
Diminishes, threatening the few species

Living on the floes of my more and more mild
Heart—the white bears that stalk feelings
Especially, are finding less and less wild

So, land-tamed and ice chipped back, fall
Into tepid water nearly warm enough to drink;
This inner tundra of my self is fraught,

As all tundra and all selves are, with caught
Nature, since natures prowl and thrive best
When least talked of and more talked through,

As if the mesh between prisoner and love
Let tongues cross between the cold grate
Without piecemeal cutting of their red kiss.

Seismic or simply a breaking off of a chunk
Of berg, then, this shift in clime, from frigid
To temperate, from morning to much too late?

And what is the flag or thermometer planted
At the beef-pink core of my claimed identity
Doing to the radius around that place,

That may or may not still be me, like waves
That radar-blip out like tea stains from the cup
Onto the paper, browning space circularly?

Can one finger of ice—an icicle maybe—
Expose itself to the frost, and be mine,
While another, cut off, tossed to dogs, lost—

Endures another winter or summer, unnamed?
This wilderness-warming is like an earthquake
Tamed, stroked down so it sleeps, a white cat

Curled against the ground, nice and flat;
The sky is flake on flake on flake of snow,
Which is all I know of winter, need to know,

For hell is ice and heaven blue sky thinking
There are clouds above. I miss my own dead,
Despite the cooling zones inside that run to spring.

Brain activity

crushed, like wrapping paper,
a damaged flowering ball
of sides and folds; no finger goes
into the there-here perceived

cupping a blank over face fronts
to hold back blind crackles
complicated unfolding sheets:
sensory rickshaw clattering over

thought-stones and felt-holes
dangle hurry deliver halt go go
the sleet fever that posts a mind
hot as knife knows butter better

so it steams the envelope aside
the eye reading its internal evidence,
green as gold is green in summer. *Or.*
Knowing nothing (try little)

of myself: a road paved by express
meander out of the way of *rien*.
Mind is what's spread inside,
a secret opened in a long wide bed.

An England

The air is active, intervening.
Outside my window, the park is green

And divisible. A girl passes.
Sorrow narrows and reduces

Whatever were the higher trespasses.
Step out of the wind and speak

With me, if you might, goddess—
What isn't pushed down in me

Heart-throbs, though bereft.
After God, then time, left, kindness

Became a requirement, but rare, still.
I've done some thinking lately.

England's cold as water ice-boxed;
Yet, sun slowly passes a hand

Across vales and lakes here
And, momentarily, a look of grace

Descends. A thought drafts up,
Feeling like a soul might, if souls

Were allowed by rigorous testing.
Cars are parked for men to mark them.

I want so much to bunch the lamps
Together in the park, a bouquet.

The Red Bathing Cap

Red bathing cap
At the edge
Of the lake.
All of her prepares
For the water
At five o'clock,
Sun reduced,
Most bathers gone.

Mother, you stood
So before me
As I read, when
You were young,
Without the long line
Of the operation
Divisive on your hip.
You swam out

Clean and strong,
For an hour, then,
Until your head was small
On the surface,
Or not visible at all,
As I would, from time
To time, look up
From *Mimesis*

Or some anthology
To make sure you hadn't
Drowned. Beautiful, tall,
You'd go directly in,
Continue, as the lake's
Black surface dulled
At evening, and flies

Prepared themselves
For the bats to come;
Your arms bringing you
Through reflections of
White-barked trees, stone,
So far, until you'd return
Shivering, to shore,
And I'd race to bring
Your towel down,

As my father built a fire.
Enwrapped, you'd stand
By it, and dry your hair.
Now, there is no fire
Here at this public place,
And Tom is dead a year.
You're older—water
Cannot keep us young

Forever—and limp
To where you start to enter.
I want to go with you tonight,
Keep pace, but you always
Swam out alone, serene.
Red cap—(brightened like
A pricked thumb)—how it goes
In and out of the going black

Steady as your pulse, a sewing
Needle, threading water
With your breathing stroke—
Is like a light, a light to me
That says the where and why
Of home, of coming home.
I'll bring your blue towel as
You stand out in summer dusk.

The Forties

Of time, the whole shivering mess
Of inhalation, of Paris,
Of what lamplight may express
Best when extinguished, how
A distinguished man will dress
Only to undress a woman under
The eye of the moon, the eyes
Of mirrors, in the hall, the spare
Room and turned to walls, to see

The damp arabesques that Poe once
Urged on decorators everywhere,
In his *Philosophy of Furniture,*
When he could not yet envisage
The opaque effects of the future.
That smell of books as good as honey
Or milk in tea, promising
A day swept clear of storms, though
Across the bay, a headland of cloud
Desires to break upon the sky

Like glass wants to step out
Of its mirror, to surprise and redraw
The angles of the day, the word's repose;
As if she was a sitter for a poet
Whose every metaphor was to curve
Her black fringe above the eyes
Away to reveal the small scars
On a scalp that was drawn away
From the womb with strong callipers.

Still beautiful, her head, despite
How it first came into the world,
Came into seeing, and being seen.
This doubling, as composed,
Rebreaks rain upon the windows
Where the house turns out over the cove,
And the night begins its trains
Across the countryside, upsetting the owls
Resuscitating the Forties with cries:
Children have cowls and *altars are wise.*

Fertility

Bolts past, and past, and through names.
History seems young beside its fluent flame—
The flower without a root, star without a start—
The reason for being early, or late,

The richest date, the opposite of zero,
The cognate's cognate, the king's bee,
The blackness of blackness being reversed,
The hero who sits up and laughs in the hearse;

The only manner in which death is cursed;
The stage on which all monkeys rehearse Lear;
The queer split shiver erupting ingots across
Time so bars of body and knowing solidify

To be born; it is the spliced film of things,
The jumpsuit, the steamboat's toot, the lute
That strings of numbers explode sideways into.
Without this fractious miracle, this intervention

No one, no mind, no skin, no lips, no eye, no one;
How the spill slip causeway goes against caution;
It outdoes eloquence, requires no passion.
Can there be such control in the spasm of the sea,

Such science in the lightning strike that crosses Z
With A, dashing across all letters, chromosome by
Chromosome, unzipping, sped by dot and hyphen,
So real it makes accidents of each, women, men,

Makes love sometimes a field of intention,
Waves of tousled, febrile, sweet information?
Its shadow is arctic nullity, the barren place
Where loss is chaste, and memory is not

Chased, across a tundra of insufficiency.
Not to be the fire but the water that shuts off fire;
Each body carrying a coin that turns on life or not;
Parenting or oblivion; to prosper or be forgotten.

We sink in skin and prepare to rot, are rotten.
I stutter here at the page of my lover like a fool
And the spirit of the piston at the level of encore
Is both stupid and crafty, beastly and jungleful.

"Send for the boys who do not care"

Send for the boys who do not care,
The rude birds that avoid the air,

The girls who shave off all their hair,
Flyers that crash down for a dare—

Send for the scribes who are impure.
Let them serve up sherbet and maize,

Warmest Florida days, a dance craze
Started in Harlem, and nothing in place,

See, there are no shoes to win this race—
Blessed are those who fail to justify

The ways in which they select high
And low manners of making desire sigh.

Mania belongs to the song of songs sung
With thrusters burning, all wheels swung

Wide to glide like butter or ice going across
A pan, out to sea which cannot adjudicate

Between a well-turned ankle and a sharp skate
But glistens like a flustered many-glozed affair.

"There is, in it"

There is, in it, something of the autumn,
Something of a lake bottom; a favour being
Returned, unopened. A letter burnt.

A lesson unlearned. A muffled oar, risking
Silence for lifting through water. Numb
Fingers reconnecting knots. Women laying out

Fuel for themselves in a damp, starlit lot.
But what is mostly in it is what is not.
Stars as they turn into their unbright coldness,

Daughters as they slide still onto the ground;
Each unborn animal, each unstruck match,
Each ambush left before the riders enter

The narrow pass. The snake that forgot
To spend its tension spilling in tall grass.
Windows no stone decided needed breaking.

The high bedroom emptied of mourners, the king
Lifted out, recovered, only to slip and fall
Next morning, and so resume a smallness

On his own. The cold floors of parliaments
After the last to cross has gone and locked a door.
The pocket watch she found, and wound

So that it said it was eleven all day round.
Its chain was golden, and it contrived a line
Across the rich lawn, gathering dew,

So that, on being brushed aside, it was rain.
A brain pivots on what is beyond it
As lies hide around the corner from coming true.

Playtime

All days are one fine day in the far sun,
So take your black parasol to the fair.
The end is what is after what's begun.

You can eat marmalade and be Shogun
Just wrap the scimitar in your bright hair.
All days are one fine day in the far sun.

Sometimes the whirlathon is just for fun.
That's why the Magnetic Man wasn't there.
The end is what is after what's begun.

Night is easily put upon, can be done.
Go and come back; click heels with care.
All days are one fine day in the far sun.

The ice was sweet, the ladder was Teflon.
If dressing, then go as a dancing bear.
The end is what is after what's begun.

They dropped the question, it weighed a ton.
She used up certain words, he said don't care.
All days are one fine day in the far sun;
The end is what is after what's begun.

Seaway

Perennial ice plagues the ships

The child is not a child but a receiver

Observe how ice is like a streetlamp

Lit in the blue night of winter, electricity

Only one form of many in which to reach far

The ships as they seek the Seaway are ice-rimed

The black tracery of the Locks opens

Receiving their lit silent transit, laden

The children sing sea-chants

Of ice-lit nights, sailing further out

Beyond the ocean, ocean, then Japan

The Lake

An arm of lightning breaks the afternoon
in half with the ease of an oar lifting light.

I rise from dreaming, my father prowls,
throwing his wild beam to the woods,

his shadow a bear's, dwelling beyond
where we'd sleep, in fear. He was worried:

thought things no one else understood:
that they would come for us.

The flashed light would sweep across my face
at midnight or at three, lifting me from sleep

and, ordered into the dew or the long webs,
I'd wander with him down the lane, silent

as Indian-hunters, each of us with a knife.
Days, he'd row out, sleep, or gather in wood

for one more night of burning, fending
off the violent men he said would visit.

I have been in this water; eaten here; slept;
awoken; had wrong visions, and been raised

to break the delicate bond that holds together
the world as it is woven by what happens,

from what never was, except in imagination:
darkness spread: forest in my father's mind.

Trees

Trees that have been there, always—
like music that cannot go away—
in any park or street of the mind,
each appearing as a dream does,
with laws only it need not obey—
going, returning with the casual powers
of wind, rain—the trees that were there,
pressing on window, on eye, in winter,
in broad day, the time walking home
or running late. How sky moved
ceremoniously in their highness,
how one fallen was a loss and omen
on a path. Will branches shade me then?—
good company in that darkening arbour.

Sleeping More

First, the sleeping, then the sleeping more.
But a sleeping spot, integral, that rolls
Through things, as a ray can a wall, a bone.
Alone is what the central place is for,

Where the I that calls itself to attention
Is often identical with nothing at all;
Fire and ice have sometimes been spoken
Of as if having sight, or vision, by reason

Of the glittering element in them, a simile;
Science cannot bend that far, no sight
Occurs in the flame, the chip of rime;
Blindness is the rose at the core of cold

And heat; a dark scroll opening its table-
Stopping sprawl, a mercurial cloth that
Folds in flame, that darts and jabs, like
A boxer in a field, facing a bare tree;

But whether it is warmth or sub-zeroing
That needs to be connected to another
Thing by writing it out, altering science,
I cannot speak of the substance within

What I try to think through as who I
Speak of being when I use a signature
That begins with a high T, falls with
That second, farther-along lower case t.

An Irish Show House on Easter Sunday

Lie down with me in the Show House
On the third floor, a floor, like all others
Under-warmed by gas—having walked in
After walking on the Flaggy Shore,
Shoes forensically capped in blue bagging.
The little blue bags of our feet wander

To explore the million euro space:
We won't get lost in the guts of luxury;
On the marble counters, blueprints
Fan out, a winning hand. There's a wide
Flat black television embedded
In the bathroom wall, electrics

Safe behind something thicker than glass.
Three wet rooms are dry as a bone,
But promise spry conventions of au pairs
With nothing much on—it's aspirational.
One young girl picks at the piano
On the landing like it was snot.

Come right up beside the telescope set
On the Master Bedroom's highest floor.
Look, see lots half-done, like dropped
Puzzles in a hospital, drugged machines
Dragging time. Stretch out here in peace
Of mind. A bloody shroud blows in a tree.

For the Camlots

Precisely because
I didn't order the lobster
Do I say now bring me more
I met two mentalists

Dining out
On their thoughts
Of their fellow
Mentalists

They were most critical
Of one guy I didn't know
But apparently he had me
Plainly in his mind

I am trying to devise
A system that can say love;
Immanence and transcendence
Are not so divided here

Both can relax in style
That split-levels
No pool can pass muster
When the mustard is spread

By a miser, who prides
The cage with sun-green lions
To save the colour yellow
From the eyes of children

So sorry that they die
And all this is the excuse
To produce excess that persists
Anywhere but where they disappear

Early Work

Not now clarity, not now.
Hold down, day job,
Steer clear. Once
Language sobbed
Teenage, Anglophone.

That screen's
Been wiped—2 bros.
Fell 66 stories—
1 lived, lying flat
The upright one dashed

To bits; a poetic.
Most feeling's preordained.
Ice enlarged itself,
A dictator's account,
Outside the window

February nights—
Mercilessly thirteen,
Fourteen, I confess
Dialled the girl-phone,
Went on and on.

Sub-zero assured
Of its grip
On the deep deep lawns,
High-banked snow.
Love's talking papers.

Form and the Line

Who can choose a line and let it stay?
The way it deepens is where it takes light.
Form is what slips through, what gets away.

A church is made to shape a sound that prays
As windows become sun-gods nearest to night.
Who can choose a line and let it stay?

Waves hold shifting land at partial bay,
Correcting, at high tide, an unequal sight.
Form is what slips through, what gets away.

Stuttering is closest to what one wants to say,
Mistakes typos run off to speaking right.
Who can choose a line and let it stay?

Paths through brambles hide bears that slay,
Slashing against dense wood starts the fight.
Form is what slips through, what gets away.

It can't be constant if it's truer might,
Good force finds outlet in cracks, the flight.
Who can choose a line and let it stay?
Form is what slips through, what gets away.

One Hundred Lines

I had come to the place,
Where, hearing talk of it,
One thinks never to reach:
The shelf lemmings dare
Bypass, books in Empson's

Earthquake quiver from,
The past-clever home
For poets, when, inkhorn
Dry, their plain pure language
Has run out, like some

Battered car in Texas,
Miles and miles from gas,
Ironic in the midst of all
The diving pens into the soil,
Those upstart, downturning

Peckers that dive for oil,
And dot the desert like a rash;
Judging by such an arid
Moonscape as a base to write,
One leans on the hood, chews

A 'pick and spits, to think
On all the vast wide space
Bequeathed to the mind,
To imagine as full of something
Else: the roaming creatures

That writing finds. A lodestone
Or lone star sort of state, depending—
But basically, blank as a cheque
From a friend who has up and died,
So you might scrawl in some line

Pretending to be them, to cash in,
But can't—your style your own
Or, following on Seneca, refined,
Or rather, naturally form-fitted
To your virtue; that is, my zoo

Animals, or was it circus, have
All petrified. They're through.
Gone daddy gone. No more
Reason for being blue or true.
Was language ever designed

Like a Hughes plane, to deliver
A verity? Seems hard to land
Such a wide-bodied claim,
Even when the land is big as sky.
What died to make words ring

With truth? To me, that idea
Pertains to the thing after words,
Or previously, a past episode.
I load my ore with outlandish
Clutter, not to bring the steer in

To brand, or land the walloping
Salmon to the shore, but to sing
A score that has no meaning other than
The sound, or even more, the fun—
That's too plain, but anyway, this voice

Chosen here is not mine, phew, glad
That confession's over—but then
Whose is it? Professor X's?
Artifice and authenticity begin the same,
In someone (or automaton) pretending

To compose by laying words on end,
An endless track from sea to sea,
On which all industry and commerce
Depend. I don't claim to be Jesse
James, or the King James version, either,

Liable to halt the engine as it sails
Across the waves of prairie, to offload
The golden insight in the big black vault.
The fault is in the chug-chug procession
Of creation, which begins to cease,

Like biological conditions of the specimen;
Organic? Didn't mean to be, believe
In quite the reverse, creation less Darwinian,
The finger-zapped instanter blast of a God
Making all everything ever at once,

Which, when written (said) sounds false,
Perhaps the reason writing is dangerous:
By putting down the line one shows
Precisely the ignorance by which one knows
What isn't true or cannot be said, what

Thoughts, before they happened, were
Not even oozing from the oil of the head.
So there's the theme I haven't had:
Two summers since I tended to my Dad,
Dying, as all do, and how mourning fed

A kind of released grandeur from my tongue;
As when I wanted poetry, when young;
Now, having stopped my sorrow
As one does, in time, I have also found
No more reason to need to rhyme;

It is the ending of the need that begins
The play—the spooling out of the spider's
Fibre strong as caution but light as day—
Enwebbed, one writes, or then is written on,
And nothing placed into the midst belongs

To evidence or witness stand—floats free—
Or hopes to, in sticky search of locking-in
The wriggling at the pit of poetry—
A smallest beast, to suck dry of its blood,
An ending better than the start is good.

End Notes and Acknowledgements

As this is a collection that represents twenty years of writing, I have many people to acknowledge, as my writing has always been open to others. The poems selected here were written and/or published between 1988 and 2008. Between 1990 and 1999 many of the early poems were collected in pamphlets and chapbooks, with titles like *The End of the Century* and *French Maid,* and then these in turn were revised and selected for *Budavox: Poems 1990-1999,* my first full collection, published by DC Books, who went on to support my poetry throughout the 00s, publishing my next three collections in Canada, as *Café Alibi* (2002), *Rue du Regard* (2004) and *Winter Tennis* (2007). The Canada Council for the Arts supported the writing of some of this poetry. I remain particularly grateful to DC series editor Robert Allen for supporting and editing my work at this time; as well as Steve Luxton, who also helpfully edited these poems at DC, and Keith Henderson.

I wish to also thank the editors of each of the following online and print publications, where many of these poems first appeared: *The Alsop Review (Octavo); Babylon Burning; Chapman; Cimarron Review; Cordite; The Cúirt Annual 2005; De Facto; Dig; Drunken Boat; The Fifteen Project; Future Welcome; The Guardian (Saturday Review); Jacket; Limelight; The Los Angeles Review; Magma; The Manhattan Review; Matrix; Natural Curve; New American Writing; The Oil and Gas University; Orbis; Other Magazine; Otherwheres; Oxford Magazine; Paper Tiger; Poetry London; Ripple; Sandstone; Seam; The Shop; Square Lake; Taiga; Tall Lighthouse Review; UEA MA Poets Anthology; Upstairs At Duroc; Vallum; west47 online;* and *The Wolf.*

The following poets—often also good friends and always good readers—read these poems and offered invaluable suggestions—not all of which I accepted: Al Alvarez, Jenna Butler, Jason Camlot, Patrick Chapman, Alfred Corn, Steven Heighton, Kevin Higgins, Luke Kennard, Roddy Lumsden, Lachlan Mackinnon, David McGimpsey, Alex McRae, Lisa Pasold, Sally Read, Clive Scott, George Szirtes, Tom Walsh, Rachel Warrington, David Wevill, and John Hartley Williams. Denise Riley has been a very special guide at UEA. I wish to register my profound gratitude to them all here.

A few other friends were guides in matters not unconnected to poetry, especially Father Brennan, Letty and Richard, Etienne Gilfillan, Dr. Sass, Martin Penny, and Thor Bishopric. Jack and Bev Swift early inspired my love of poetry and drama. My mother and father read and sang to me as a child, sparking all my poems. My beloved wife Sara Egan has helped more than any other.

I have made corrections to, and otherwise revised, several of the earlier poems here, to achieve the effects I could not then. These are meant to be the definitive versions, until further notice.

"Ocean, ocean, then Japan" is a paraphrase of a line by Milosz.

The dedication and care with which Jessie Lendennie and Siobhán Hutson oversaw the preparation of this book is most appreciated.

Finally, special thanks to poet Siobhán Campbell, who suggested the title of this collection.

About the Author

Todd Swift was born in Montreal, Quebec, Canada, on Good Friday, 1966, and grew up in St-Lambert. He was one of Canada's top-ranked student debaters throughout high school and university. He graduated with a BA in English and Creative Writing from Concordia University. In the 1990s he helped develop spoken word in Canada, with his poetry cabarets. His CD-length experimental text-music collaboration with Tom Walsh, *Swifty Lazarus: The Envelope, Please,* was released by Wired On Words in 2002. A graduate of the MA in Creative Writing at UEA, he is core tutor with The Poetry School, and a lecturer in creative writing and English literature at Kingston University. His recent collection of critical essays about Anglo-Quebec poetry, *Language Acts,* co-edited with Jason Camlot, was a finalist for the 2007 Gabrielle Roy Prize. His poems have appeared in the major anthologies *The New Canon* and *Open Field*; and his poem "Gentlemen of Nerve" was selected to appear in *The Best Canadian Poetry in English, 2008.* He is the editor of many significant international poetry anthologies, including *Poetry Nation, Short Fuse,* and *100 Poets Against The War;* and is the poetry editor of *Nthposition.* In 2005, he edited a special section on The Young Canadian Poets for *New American Writing.* He has had four full collections of poems published by DC Books in Montreal. As Oxfam Great Britain's first Poet-in-residence, 2004-2008, he ran the influential Oxfam Poetry Series, and edited the best-selling CDs, *Life Lines* and *Life Lines 2—Poets for Oxfam.* In 1997, Swift moved to Budapest, then to Paris in 2001. He now lives and works in London, England, with his Irish wife, Sara.